The
SPORTING
SEASON

A
Celebration
of the
British Sporting Year
2001

Publishers Acknowledgements

The Sporting Season™

Copyright © 2001 The Sporting Season Limited

First Edition

Published in Great Britain, in 2001, by

The Sporting Season Limited,
PO Box 332,
Huntingdon, PE28 3RX
Telephone 01487 824466
E-mail: enquiries@thesportingseason.com
The Sporting Season website www.thesportingseason.com

ISBN 0-9539758-0-0

Designed by
20/20 Image
Telephone 020 8424 0022

Photographs supplied by Allsport UK Limited (see picture credits page 126)
Polo, by Hugo Burnand and Tim Griffiths.

Printed in Denmark

The Sporting Season supports SPARKS (Sport Aiding medical Research for Kids)
50p from each copy sold will go to support the vital work of the charity.
Registered Charity NO. 100 38 25

Britain is simply the most wonderful sporting grandstand imaginable, stretching from the Six Nations in Winter, the Grand National in early Spring, through to the Alfred Dunhill Links Championship in the mists of Autumn.

And between those events, the envy of the sporting world, the Mecca for sporting followers from many countries – Wimbledon and the Lord's Test, Royal Ascot and Cowes Week, the British Formula One Grand Prix and the Derby, and so much else. We simply do not provide the vantage point, but the winners as well – the incomparable Redgrave, the duelling Montgomerie to name but two.

This is the story of the season ahead, of events past and of glories to come. The season is, of course, a social festivity as well, a place to feast and to be seen. This book is not just the story of the social whirl. It is the story of the sportsmen and women, of the controversies and triumphs and of the growth of traditions at the various venues. It is the story of competition at its most galvanising, and sport at its least leisurely.

THE SPORTING SEASON

Contents

Veuve Clicquot

CHAMPAGNE OF THE SEASON

The Lloyds TSB

Six Nations

Championship

GAVIN HASTINGS - *former Scottish & British Lions Captain*

The Six Nations Championship remains firmly at the forefront of the rugby season in the northern hemisphere. It's history and tradition is something that is unique in world sport and our southern hemisphere cousins, despite the success of the Super 12's and Tri-Nations, look enviously at the position the Six Nations holds in the winter sporting calendar.

Italy's astonishing start to their inaugural season amongst Europe's elite last year was just what was required with victory against defending champions Scotland. Their challenge in the years ahead is to keep remaining competitive whilst building up their playing and supporter base so that a one-off victory is not seen as an upset.

Rome as a place to visit certainly adds further colour to the delights of Cardiff, London, Edinburgh, Dublin and Paris where supporters have travelled in their tens of thousands over the years to renew friendships and retell stories of past sporting encounters.

The mythical Triple Crown and Grand Slam were what each team aspired to prior to the introduction of the Five Nations Trophy a few years ago. This is awarded of course to the team coming out on top whilst not necessarily winning all their games. Prior to that the Championship would be tied if two or more teams had the same number of victories. No points differential was included.

Times have moved on and the switch to professionalism in the late summer of 1995 meant that rugby at the top level was to change for ever. For the diehards perhaps it was for the worst but for others there was a huge opportunity to be exploited. There's no doubt that it was grasped firmly by our friends in the Southern Hemisphere first and although we have been playing catch up ever since there are signs that we are getting closer. England and France both recorded victories against Australia and New Zealand in their preparation for this years Six Nations while Scotland, Wales, Ireland and Italy enjoyed success against only the lesser lights of Samoa, USA, Japan and Romania.

The uniqueness of the Six Nations is such that different playing styles in each country contrast to produce classic confrontations with a favourites tag being almost as much use as a noose around the neck. How many times have we witnessed an upset and seen the underdog throwing caution to the wind and playing with a confidence that totally belied their lowly status.

Both Wales and Scotland have dented the Grand Slam hopes of England in recent years in the last game of the Championship, which shows just how difficult winning away from home really is. Ireland though achieved just that when they recorded their historic victory over France in Paris last year, whilst Italy achieved more than they dared to hope for in Rome at the first time of asking.

Europe's premier tournament, because of such drama and uncertainty, is unrivalled in world rugby. The interest from players and spectators alike shows no signs of abating. Whatever is achieved during the Autumn Internationals is a one off with no carry forward to the next match and no tournament to be won.

The Six Nations Championship which this year spans thirteen weeks requires each nation to produce a consistency of performance. Playing conditions, injuries, team selection and individual form can vary wildly throughout the February to April period. Whichever team comes closest to mastering the unique demands placed upon them is well entitled to call themselves Champions of Europe.

Let battle commence!

Matches start on Saturday 3rd February through to Sunday 8th April 2001 and will be held at the following venues:

Twickenham	Plas de Parc
London	75431 Paris
TW1 1DS	France
Murrayfield	62 Lansdowne Road\Balls
EH12 5PJ	Bridge
Scotland	Dublin 4
	Ireland
Millennium Stadium	
Cardiff	Salminio Stadium
CF10 1RF	Rome
Wales	Italy

The *National Hunt*
Festival Cheltenham

RICHARD DUNWOODY - *Former National Hunt Champion and Grand National Winner*

Cheltenham is the home of Steeplechasing. This racecourse has particular relevance to my career as I rode my first ever winner there on Game Trust on May 4th, 1983 and I returned in 1994 to ride my 1,000th winner on the great mare Flakey Dove in 1994.

For every jockey the Cheltenham Festival is the highlight of the season. Every race is hard to win but no more so than at the Cheltenham Festival and especially The Gold Cup. This race is quite special and the roar of the crowd, augmented by thousands of my fellow Irishmen is unrivalled.

The horses that go down in National Hunt racing legend; Arkle, Cottage Rake, Golden Miller, Sea Pigeon and Dawn Run are synonymous with Prestbury Park, the racecourse at Cheltenham. The latest addition to the list includes Istabraq after his third consecutive win in last year's Champion Hurdle. Amazingly it was fifty years earlier that Cottage Rake took his record-breaking third Gold Cup, trained on the same gallops in Ballydoyle, Ireland as Istabraq.

I retired from race riding in December 1999 on doctor's orders having ridden a total of 1699 winners. I had, in all 12 rides in the Gold Cup. My greatest memory is of course when I rode the winner of this spectacle.

Charter Party winning The Gold Cup in 1988 was undoubtedly one of the highlights of my career. The horse was probably one of the most underrated I ever rode. Many people said that year's race was not a vintage one but never once have I ridden in a bad Cheltenham Gold Cup. Were it not for persistently niggling problems Charter Party had with his legs and feet, he would, I am sure been one of the greatest steeplechasers of that

decade. His problems were epitomised when I mounted him on that glorious day when his stable lad, Tommy said to me 'He hasn't taken a lame step all day'!

Though Charter Party's race was wonderful for personal reasons, the best and most exciting Gold Cup I ever saw was the win of Anne, Duchess of Westminster's Dawn Run's in 1986. Apart from being an exceptionally popular mare both here and in Ireland she was 15-8 favourite and was supported by most of the punters. I was having my first ride in the race and fell at the fourth last on Von Trappe. There is a slight drop in the fence and it caught him out. I got myself up off the ground and watched the finish of the race from the top of the hill on the opposite side of the course.

I couldn't see the field, just the stands packed with the crowd. As the runners turned into the home straight there was an almighty cheer as Dawn Run and her jockey Jonjo O'Neil began to make their run, the mare looked to be beaten at the second last and there was suddenly an eerie silence. Then, of course, when they had jumped the last and she began to get up to defeat Wayward Lad the whole place exploded once again. I've never heard a noise like it before or again since. When Dawn Run passed the line literally thousands of caps and hats were thrown in the air. When I arrived back at the weighing room Jonjo was being led in, mobbed by the crowd and was very nearly dragged from the mare on several occasions.

The Gold Cup is the Blue Riband of steeplechasing and it's equivalent over hurdles is of course the Champion Hurdle. I was lucky enough to capture this prize in 1990 on the enigmatic grey, Kribensis. The horse was, interestingly trained by the champion flat trainer Sir Michael Stoute and owned by the all conquering Sheikh Mohammed.

As an Irishman some of my fondest memories of The Festival are when I triumphed aboard horses trained in my native land. Especially when gambled on, the reception one receives being lead into the winners enclosure on an Irish horse is unrivalled. I received such an ovation on horses like Montelado in the Bumper and Florida Pearl in the Sun Alliance Novice Chase.

The Gold Cup remains undoubtedly the pinnacle of the National Hunt year but it is worth remembering that however short priced the favourite, anything can happen, as 100-1 winner Norton's Coin proved in 1990!

EVENT

The National Hunt Festival Cheltenham

ADDRESS

Prestbury Park Cheltenham Race Course Cheltenham Gloucestershire GL50 4SH

EVENT DATE

13th - 15th March 2001

WINNERS IN 2000

Looks Like Trouble Ridden by Richard Johnson (Gold Cup)

TICKETS & INFORMATION

01242 226226

Sportsworld Hospitality Line 01235 555844

WEB SITES

www.cheltenham.co.uk

For Hotel, Weather, Travel Directions and Additional Information Visit www.thesportingseason.com

NAUTICA

The *Boat Race*

DANIEL TOPOLSKI - *Former Oxford Blue, Coach & Commentator*

Rowing has gone through a sea change in popularity and public awareness since Steve Redgrave secured his coveted fifth Olympic title in Sydney last year. Seven million people stayed up after midnight to watch his race on television – a record for late night TV audiences.

But until Redgrave came along the Oxford and Cambridge Boat Race was the only rowing event that most people in this country were aware of and watched every year. The annual domestic television audiences for this gruelling marathon Varsity battle on the Thames vary between seven and ten million on the day.

What we should not forget though is that rowing with Redgrave in that triumphant four were two graduates of the Boat Race –

Matthew Pinsent, a three times Oxford Blue and ex President of the club, and Tim Foster who stroked Oxford four years ago. In that fine Eights performance the next day – Britain's first victory in this blue riband event since 1912 – were two more former Boat Race men: Andrew Lindsay who rowed for Oxford for three years and Kieran West who won with Cambridge in 1999. He will be back in Light Blue colours again for this years race. And rowing in the fourth placed Olympic Pair was Ed Coode, another Oxford graduate. A third then of Britain's heavyweight men's team were past Boat Race men.

Sponsored by Aberdeen Asset Management with a world wide TV and radio audience of 400 million, the Varsity race produces a fine return on their investment. This year Cambridge are hoping to return to their winning ways and extend their lead in the series to 77 against Oxford's 69. Apart

from West they have three Blues from last year and most of their reserve crew while Oxford, less star studded and younger, have five Blues and two reserve crew men. Both squads have a number of new freshmen with Cambridge appearing the stronger contenders – on paper at least.

But the Boat Race, if it is anything, is unpredictable which is what gives it its unique flavour. Oxford won against the odds last year in a memorable race, ending a seven-year period of Cambridge dominance. Before that Cambridge had won but twice in nineteen years since 1974. It was though a rare Dark Blue phase. Cambridge's success before that was so great that their toast every year was 'Please God let Oxford win, but not this year!' Oxford won only 12 races out of the 60 between 1914 and 1973.

The ever-present possibility of a sinking or a collapsing oarsman – the hint of imminent disaster – adds a special frisson to the contest. But last year's neck and neck battle was a demonstration of just how tough a race it really is. Remember too the spine chilling 6 foot win by Oxford in 1980 when Cambridge clawed back a two length deficit over the final mile. Two years before that they sank within sight of the finish.

The six-month build-up too is often peppered with incident. Cambridge threatened to pull out when five times Dark Blue winner Boris Rankov was selected for his sixth race in 1983. After a long wrangle they capitulated. Sue Brown became the first woman to take part and in 1981 rivalled Princess Diana for media attention. And in 1987 a group of American internationals mutinied and seized control of the club because they were not prepared to do the amount of training needed to win a Boat Race. Donald MacDonald, the President, became a folk hero as he fought a two-month rear guard action to win back control and then led a much-weakened crew to an extraordinary and wholly unexpected victory. The film of the book of the mutiny was the 1998 Royal Command Performance show attended by H.M. The Queen and HRH Prince Philip. The training programme that daunted the mutineers was common practice for internationals and Boat Race rowers then and is no less taxing now.

Crucially though, both universities now employ full time managers and professional coaches. Before sponsorship was introduced to provide financial security, unpaid former participants in the race and keen amateur supporters covered the coaching. The rowers themselves had to deal with daily transport arrangements and all logistical problems as well as

their 5 hours of training, all of which was inefficient, tiring and time-consuming. Now the clubs operate well-organised systems. The equipment they use is little changed although plastic and carbon composite lightweight oars as well as boats are now the norm. There is also a fuller range of athletic aides like rate and pulse meters; and medical testing becomes more sophisticated every year. Oxford used the first British produced plastic eights in the late 70's and the legendary post war coach Jumbo Edwards was forever experimenting in his workshop.

The event is a high-class show case for the sport attracting big sponsorship and regularly offering up Olympic class athletes; (4 Oxbridge Blues struck gold in Sydney) and the Boat Race is the only university sport that has kept pace with international standards. In training fixtures during most years the Varsity crews race level with the British eight designate, and although London University's national team members would like to claim superiority, it is rare that they are faster.

For those individuals there is no money to be won, no advertising endorsements to earn, not even the adoration of sporting groupies. The very nature of this uniquely team sport denies them star status. They must submit themselves and their individuality to the benefit of the crew. No one stands out, for to do so is to upset the rhythm of the boat, the smooth and fluent flow of their joint effort.

There is a gritty 'mad dogs and Englishmen' feel about it all which represents something uniquely British. They face a cruel 4.25 miles of rough and windswept Thames in March – the most inhospitable time of the year – winding and treacherous and three times the official international distance of 2,000 metres which is always on a straight buoyed six lane course. Unfair? Of course it's unfair. That is what makes it such an endurance test. That is why tactics play such an important role to capture the fastest stream and to work the bends in your favour. That is why the fastest crew does not always win.

In all other sporting life you can race in heats and play your game for as long as you like, make a career out of it gaining experience and strength while suffering all the triumphs and defeats of competition. But in the Boat Race there is only that one singular climax that matters, which suspends your life for those twenty grim yet life-enhancing minutes and which gives meaning and resonance to all the months and years of training that have gone before. There is nothing else in the world quite like it and it is a moment that lives with the Boat Race Blue forever.

EVENT

The Boat Race sponsored by Aberdeen Asset Management

ADDRESS

Start - Putney SW15
Half way - Hammersmith Bridge SW13
Finish - Chiswick Bridge SW14

EVENT DATE

24th March 2001

WINNERS IN 2000

Oxford

TICKETS & INFORMATION

020 7465 7037
Sportsworld Hospitality Line 01235 555844

WEB SITES

www.cubc.org.uk
www.oubc.rowing.org.uk
For Hotel, Weather, Travel Directions and Additional Information Visit
www.thesportingseason.com

The Martell
Grand National

MARCUS ARMYTAGE - *Winner in 1990 on Mr Frisk*

In 1835 William Lynn, a publican in Liverpool, had an idea that a steeplechase near his prospering town might not only be popular with the locals but more importantly for him, a useful additional source of income. Little can he have imagined that he was founding a national institution, the greatest event of its kind in the world and a race renowned for its characters and fairytales, as popular now in Britain as it is with its worldwide audience.

The Grand National was probably first run in 1837 although there is some dispute about this. Some historians refer to Lottery's success in 1839 as the inaugural National. However, the make and shape of the race has changed considerably during its 156-year history. In those early days the obstacles were not much more than 2ft high banks although by the 1880's Becher's Brook was 9ft 6in wide and 6ft deep.

The public clamour for radical alterations to Becher's Brook in 1989 following the death of two horses at the fence was tame by comparison to the hostile demands for a parliamentary Bill to make Aintree safer in 1928. Then, a 20 horse pile up at the Canal Turn left 100-1 shot Tipperary Tim to come home in virtual solitude. As a result the 6ft wide ditch preceding the fence into which a loose horse had turned broadside to the field causing the melee, was filled in for the 1931 race.

Alterations since have been to both the course itself and to the conditions of entry. Raising the standard of runner and rider by tightening qualifications has undoubtedly had a beneficial effect on the safety of the race although at a cost of some characters. The Duque d'Albequeque, who annually had a bed reserved for him on the night after the National in Walton Hospital, would probably have been prevented from riding now on medical grounds. Some modifications like replacing wooden or steel fencing and railing with plastic rails and draining large tracts of the course make no visual difference to Aintree but have contributed enormously to improved safety, although the number of finishers nearly always reflects the underfoot conditions. The softer or heavier the ground the fewer the finishers.

Major changes since 1931 have included the addition of spruce aprons to each fence, a sloping rather than upright obstacle being more inviting to both horse and rider. Tragically the engineer of Aintree's latest alterations, John Parrett, died out hunting in the 1990s cruelly denying him the chance to guide the race as he undoubtedly would have done with great success into the 21st Century. But he handled what had been a difficult time for Aintree, pressure from animal rights on the one hand and tradition, conservative racing fans on the other with diplomacy, common sense and prompt action.

He accepted public unease about Becher's Brook – we're living in a time when racing has to respond to adverse criticism – and levelled the backward slope into the ditch on the landing side. 'Maintaining the standard but reducing the price of failure' he

said. There were those of us who thought it akin to bulldozing a wing of Buckingham Palace. The photos of Becher's may not be as spectacular as they used to be but the non-racing crowds were placated. The fence is unquestionably safer and now, given a year or two and most have forgotten what the old Becher's was like. Personally, I don't think it jumps like it used to although, having said that, it still claimed the one horse that stood between Mr Frisk and my victory, Uncle Merlin, in 1990.

One major change is unquantifiable. That is the stiffness of the fences. They remain pretty much the same height, average 5ft. During the early 1990s I am convinced they became a bit softer and horses were able to get away with hitting them lower and getting away without a fall. Now they take a great deal of jumping again and though we are not back to the black and white Movietone days of the 1950s when they were like brick walls they are back to what they were like during Red Rum's seventies. One of the challenges of Aintree was that it required impeccable jumping and it still does.

Yet, despite the changes and the fact that the Grand National no longer has jockeys quaking in their boots, it remains different from any other race. It is a race apart and the one that every jockey, trainer and owner wishes, above all else, to win. Horses with an entry in the race or a good chance quite often change hands for vastly inflated prices, sometimes several times their true value. The best case of this was Party Politics who changed hands on the eve of his success in 1992 for a small fortune. He had had a history of severe breathing problems and it is unlikely, had he not been fancied for the National, that anyone would have bought him. As it was he went on to become the most successful Aintree horse since Red Rum and gave his new owners more than value for money.

As a breed jump jockeys do not have the same sporting stature as international footballers or cricketers. However the National remains, perhaps more so now with the increased media coverage of the major sporting events of the calendar, a 10 minute ride to immortality, if not in sport in general then at least within racing. That first Saturday in April belongs to Aintree, its horses and its jockeys. It is headlines for a day. It is the only horse race that achieves a television audience that puts it in the category of major world sporting events. So much so that I'm constantly reminded that whatever else I achieve in my life my obituary will kick off with the fact that I won a Grand National.

EVENT

The Martell
Grand National

ADDRESS

Aintree Racecourse Co. Ltd.
Ormiskirk Road
Aintree
Liverpool
L9 5AS

EVENT DATE

5th - 7th April 2001
Grand National on the 7th

WINNERS IN 2000

Papillon
Ridden by
Ruby Walsh

TICKETS & INFORMATION

0151 522 2929
Sportsworld Hospitality Line
01235 555844

WEB SITES

www.aintree.co.uk

For Hotel, Weather,
Travel Directions and
Additional Information
Visit
www.thesportingseason.com

JAVLIN

British manufacturers of quality performance clothing which Takes you Anywhere Anytime.

Javlin International Limited, Sheffield S7 2BQ
Telephone 0114 2557413 E-mail: sales@javlin.co.uk Web site: www.javlin.co.uk

The Mitsubishi Motors *Badminton* Horse Trials

GINNY ELLIOT (LENG) - *Former World and European Champion*

Mention the name Badminton and the pulse quickens. Whether you are a rider or spectator, the place to be in the first week of May is on the Duke of Beaufort's beautiful Gloucestershire estate. Badminton is to Three Day Eventing as Wimbledon is to Tennis, Lord's to Cricket and Ascot to Racing. The world's best three day event riders will be competing in the season's first four star event and the crowds will flock to witness the drama and the glory of one of the most fearsome cross-country courses in existence. Second only to the Indy 500 motor extravaganza, Badminton has the biggest spectator attendance of any sporting event in the world with more than 250,000 visitors over the three days of competition. They never

leave disappointed, whether it is with memories of having seen the best horse and riders in action or with bag loads of shopping from the largest shopping mall of trade stands at any country fair in England.

Badminton is steeped in Eventing history. List the great riders of the last fifty years and most will be found on the role of honour at Badminton. It attracts riders from all over the world and the results are followed closely by absent enthusiasts from every country imaginable. Last year, the Badminton website had 3 million 'hits' over the few days of competition and more than 135,000 people downloaded the video clips of daily highlights from the Internet.

Dreams of Badminton must account for millions of hours sleeping time. Every aspiring event rider claims that their ambition is to ride over the Badminton fences. If they make the required grade, then most days of late winter and early spring are focused on getting both horse and rider prepared mentally and physically for the first major test of the season. This test is probably the most severe of the year as there has been little time for the horse and rider partnership to iron out early season problems before entering the pressure cauldron of the Badminton parkland. It is perhaps this early position in the Eventing calendar that maintains Badminton's continued prominence in everybody's mind. Badminton is the first major event of the year for riders who have achieved the required experience to ride in a Four Star competition. These riders have the added pressure in

that Badminton is the recognised proving ground for Olympic, European or World Championship selection, with those competitions always taking place in late summer. The more established riders have their own pressures in that Badminton provides their first opportunity to prove an inexperienced horse in four star company. The size of the crowds, the intensity of noise and presence of television cameras are experiences that young horses are unlikely to have encountered at lesser events. A good introduction here could be the making of a future equine star and a passport to further glory.

Badminton 2001 is likely to be the springboard for one or more very promising riders to make the final step up to stardom and national selectors will be scrutinizing all results carefully. A clear cross-country round is essential. The old guard are bowing out and there is room at the top for new names, with Great Britain having more than its share of contenders. The wonderful performance of the British Team at the Sydney Olympics could have been a serious portent for the future. Pippa Funnell, Leslie Law and Jeanette Brakewell should have several years of competition ahead of them and all have the potential to make the last leap to fame... riches are sadly not part of this particular sport, with sponsorship as hard as ever to attract and prize money unlikely to cover

the cost of keep for even the most successful team of horses. This is an expensive sport to pursue and its very existence is dependent on the generous support of enthusiasts.

Hugh Thomas has overseen the course building and development of this unique event for the past 12 years and has maintained the rich Badminton traditions, while quietly ensuring customer satisfaction for spectators, television viewers and competitors. This is not an easy formula to juggle. The public demands excitement and spectacle for their money, which is desperately needed for the continuance of this discipline. The Badminton fences have remained a proper test for the best of the best, while their construction and the setting have ensured spectacular viewing. The Lake fences have huge audience appeal and the backdrop of Badminton House make this a unique venue for all concerned.

A long range forecast for the victory parade must include the aforementioned British trio of Funnell, Law and Brakewell. The massive experience of Blyth Tait, Mary King, Ian Stark, William Fox-Pitt, Andrew Hoy and Andrew Nicholson will be invaluable to their own chances, but the rising stars are waiting to take their turn. In particular, Australian Paul Tappner had notable British success in 2000, while the young Greek rider Heidi Antikatsides will have benefited enormously from her experiences in Sydney. The Irish Olympic team included some very promising young riders and horses. With the new wealth of that country, the best of their horses will now be retained rather than sold, which will inevitably boost their performance as it has done with their showjumping team.

Whoever collects the spectacular trophy of three silver horse and riders, the real winner will be Badminton whose name will endure long after the equine and human celebrities are forgotten.

EVENT

The Mitsubishi Motors
Badminton Horse Trials

ADDRESS

Badminton
Gloucestershire
GL9 1DF

EVENT DATE

3rd - 6th May 2001

WINNERS IN 2000

Mary King
riding Star Appeal

TICKETS & INFORMATION

01454 218375

Sportsworld Hospitality Line
01235 555844

WEB SITES

www.badminton-horse.co.uk

For Hotel, Weather,
Travel Directions and
Additional Information
Visit
www.thesportingseason.com

HARRODS LUXURY HAMPERS, PERFECT FOR ANY OCCASION.

Hampers and Gift Boxes, Ground Floor. Harrods Limited, Knightsbridge, London SW1X 7XL. Telephone 020 7730 1234. www.harrods.com

Wentworth
Golf Club

The Volvo PGA Championship &
The Cisco World Match Play Championship

BERNARD GALLACHER - *Former Ryder Cup Captain and Resident Professional*

Wentworth has been my home course since 1969 – the year Tom Haliburton asked me to join him as assistant. That was the year I played my first Ryder Cup and topped the money list with nearly £70,000. My stroke average in 1969 when the Tour had not yet embraced Europe was 71.96. Curiously 22 years later I was averaging 70.64 in Volvo Tour events and finishing outside the top 150! Times have changed and Wentworth has, too, but the reputation the club has is one of the country's best inland courses, venue now of the Volvo PGA Championship and Cisco World Match Play Championship. Can it be so long since Neil Coles and Arnold Palmer fought out the first final? Mark McCormack, the entrepreneur, had seen the potential of Wentworth as the correct venue for the annual autumn head-to-head clash of golfing giants.

In the Spring, the Volvo PGA Championship can claim an impressive list of winners – a tribute to the golf course which Chris Kennedy and his green keeping staff keep in immaculate condition, helped nowadays by the extensive capital cost of

installing a fully integrated and totally computerised fairway
watering system – just one example of the continuing upgrading
of the three Wentworth courses and of the clubhouse.

Wentworth has an international reputation. It is as well known
as Cypress Point, Augusta, Royal Melbourne because of the
television exposure it gets twice a year and because so many
great players have competed at Wentworth where the Ryder Cup
was born in the 20's and the first Curtis Cup was played!

The course has always been good to me, although I have never
been able to win there.

In 1968 Brian Hugget won the Daks title but in the final round
I had a three over par 7 at the third hole and finished 6,6
against the par of 5,5! I had to be content with second place
and subsequently have been third in the World Match Play and
fifth in the PGA Championship when it was sponsored by
Viyella.

I was just 22 when I joined Tom Haliburton with no thoughts
of becoming a club professional. I was a tour player and have
remained a regular competitor, but a cruel twist of fate gave me
an earlier than expected chance to take over the running of the
professional's shop when Tom died in my arms on the first
green on the East course on a Saturday afternoon when we had
gone out to play a few holes together. I suspect he had lined me
up as his successor and, despite my age, the club was happy to
nominate me as Tom's successor in 1976.

Over the years I managed two holes in one – with a 7-iron at
the 2nd hole on the West course and the 12th on the East when
I used a 9-iron. Incidentally, it was the 2nd hole on the West
that proved a real bonus hole for Japan's Isao Aoki in the World
Match Play in 1980. He also aced there and won a luxury home
at Gleneagles Hotel which he later; I am told, sold on to his
manager, Mark McCormack.

The World Match Play has thrown up some intriguing low-
scoring clashes. There was Lee Trevino's match with Tony
Jacklin in 1972 when Jacklin played the second 18 holes in an
astonishing nine under par 63 and still lost!

One of the most intriguing matches was the tournament's 21st birthday clash of Seve Ballesteros and Arnold Palmer. The match was on the 18th and Arnold was through the green to the back fringe. It was a great shot because the pin was at the back. Seve was 90 yards short in two and in the rough....... but he holed out for 3, won the hole and squared the match. I can still see the look on Arnold's face when the ball went in. Seve won at the 19th.

In 1980, when Sandy Lyle and I were in the field, the press made much of the fact that if I beat Greg Norman in my semi-final and Sandy beat Peter Jacobsen in his semi, the final would be between Gallacher and Lyle who just happened to be a top pop group at that time! It did not happen. Sandy won but I lost 6 and 5 to Greg who went on to take the first of his three titles.

One of the most dramatic finals happened in 1989 when Nick Faldo beat Ian Woosnam on the last green. Faldo had been three down with seven to play but covered the last seven holes in seven under and indeed trimmed the back nine to a brilliant 30! During the week he was 38-under par for the 105 holes he played against Woosnam's previous record 32 under for 141 holes when he had won the title in 1987 by beating Sandy Lyle!

Great scoring on a far from easy golf course which was designed by famous Harry Colt, who also designed Sunningdale, and which has more than stood the test of time. Each hole has produced its own drama over the years. Dramatic shot making, titanic struggles, contretemps with referees, balls mystifyingly re-appearing from the gallery, structural changes and so much more. In short, it is a great test.

I count myself very fortunate to be the professional at Wentworth whose officials were delighted to make it possible for me to accept the captaincy of the European Ryder Cup team. Not surprising perhaps because it was at Wentworth in the 20's that Samuel Ryder was persuaded to present to the PGA the beautiful Gold trophy we will play the Americans for this year.

Wentworth is steeped in history and tradition, it remains one of the finest tests of golf in Britain and it will produce another quality winner in both this year's Volvo PGA Championship and Cisco World Match Play Championship.

EVENT

The Volvo
PGA Championship

ADDRESS

Wentworth Golf Club
Wentworth Drive
Virginia Water
Surrey
GU25 4LS

EVENT DATE

25th - 28th May 2001

WINNERS IN 2000

Lee Westwood

TICKETS & INFORMATION

01344 840400

Sportsworld Hospitality Line
01235 555844

WEB SITES

www.europeantour.com

For Hotel, Weather,
Travel Directions and
Additional Information
Visit
www.thesportingseason.com

EVENT

The Cisco
WorldMatch Play
Championship

ADDRESS

Wentworth Golf Club
Wentworth Drive
Virginia Water
Surrey
GU25 4LS

EVENT DATE

11th - 14th October 2001

WINNERS IN 2000

Lee Westwood

TICKETS & INFORMATION

020 8233 5000

Sportsworld Hospitality Line
01235 555 844

WEB SITES

www.cisco.com\uk\matchplay

For Hotel, Weather,
Travel Directions and
Additional Information
Visit
www.thesportingseason.com

Lord's
The Tests Matches

DAVID GOWER - *Former England Cricket Captain and Broadcaster*

I love going to any major sporting venue to savour the atmosphere that goes with every great sporting moment. It matters not that the sport in question might be one of which I have little intimate knowledge, for much of the excitement comes merely from the natural enthusiasm of any big crowd. There is also the sociable side to these events that should not be ignored, even by the strongest sporting diehard determined not to miss a moment of the day's sport; after all, if those lovely people from Bollinger have taken the trouble to set up the relevant facilities, it strikes me as churlish to ignore them!

Thus, it is that I always do my best to find a day or two each summer to get to Wimbledon, find it hard to turn down tickets to Twickenham, and even found myself one year watching ice hockey in Calgary's Saddledome during the winter Olympics, an experience that still sticks firmly in the memory banks, more so than any number of the games of cricket I have been involved in, and I had no particular allegiance to either of the two sides that night: the United States and Czechoslovakia.

As far as my own sport is concerned, however, I will always have a very soft spot for the world's premier ground, Lord's. Melbourne and Calcutta will always be able to argue that they have had the world's biggest crowds, and Sydney can lay claim to an awful lot of cricketing history (and would be my second choice as a favourite ground in the world), but Lord's is the ground where all the world's cricketers would love to play, even if only given the one chance.

The current St John's Wood site is not the first. Thomas Lord's first chosen site lies underneath what is now Dorset Square, before the ground moved to a position half a mile or so south of today's stadium. The new Regents Park canal put paid to that, in preparation for which Lord's moved for the final time in 1811. Nowadays it is the long established home of the MCC and also of the TCCB.

Technically speaking the MCC have little direct influence on the running of the game either domestically or internationally, though they do own the ground and maintain strict control over the traditions that are associated with the "home of cricket". The Test and County Cricket Board have jurisdiction over English cricket, presiding over all County cricket, and being

"responsible" for the England team and its management round the world.

From the player's point of view, nothing much will beat the thrill of finding your way down the right number of stairs to walk out onto the hallowed turf to make your first appearance there. David Steel, the former Northants and England batsman on his Test debut at Lord's apparently found himself heading for the Gentlemen's convenience in the basement instead of the field: he had just taken one flight of stairs too many!

I made my maiden first class century on this ground, for Leicestershire against Middlesex, just prior to heading off to the West Indies with an England Under 19 team. It might not have been my best ever but, as far as I was concerned, it was not a bad start. But there is no doubt that ultimate dream, at least allied to this particular topic, must be to score that hundred for England against Australia or vice versa.

The combination is unsurpassable: the Ashes also retain an air of magic and inspire the players, the media, and the supporters of both countries to abnormal levels of enthusiasm, so that if I were to pick an innings of mine at Lord's to savour, I would go for my hundred against Australia in 1989. We came to the Monday morning

under pressure as a team, Robin Smith and I really needing to bat for two days to save the game. I had upset our press corps on Saturday night by abandoning the press conference very quickly and heading for the theatre, so had an added incentive to do well and regain some lost ground.

As it happened I got my hundred, and Robin 96 and, unfortunately, the game slipped away from us in any case, but for which this would have been an ideal story.

Lord's has many stories to tell over the years but in recent years the man who seems to have got on best there is Graham Gooch, who has been prolific there. He was at his greediest against India in 1990, firstly helping himself to a gentle 333 and then going on to make another hundred in the second innings as well, to at least create a record for individual runs in a Test Match. Not only that, but on that occasion he also had the satisfaction of winning the match.

One must not fall into the trap of believing that Lord's is just for the players, vital though they are to events on the field. The history of Lord's is as much about the Long Room, with its collection of paintings and memorabilia, the Museum with more of the same in greater quantity, including the original Ashes themselves, the Committee rooms where decisions both good and bad have been taken over the years, not to mention debates on such poignant matters as "Bodyline" in the twenties, and the famous Tavern, similarly the venue for many years dominated the Committee Room that lies beneath the home dressing room and virtually abuts the stand which now bears his name. Upstairs in Q on the same level as the dressing room, is an area where the cognoscenti of the twin arts of cricket and Pimms like to meet – or at least that is my observation over several years crowd watching.

Elsewhere, the new Mound Stand is my favourite, combining aesthetics with capacity and some especially sweeping views from the debenture seats at the very top.

It has been joined now by a new Grandstand and, of course, by the completely revolutionary new media centre. It is an extraordinary and very comfortable creation, from which to broadcast – full marks to the MCC Committee for its bravery in commissioning and building it.

Don't forget to bring all the right tickets if you wish to gain entry to any part of the ground, whether you are playing or not. There are legion examples of over zealous officials barring entry to some of the game's most eminent practitioners: Sunil Gavaskar, Test cricket's leading scorer at the time of writing, failed to gain entry not so long ago and declined to accept honorary membership of the club as a result. Likewise, Clive Radley, the Middlesex stalwart also found himself barred at the gates – and he's only been playing for the county for about 20 years by then! I was wearing full whites during the MCC Bicentenary Test and tried to get up to

the Mound Stand boxes to see some friends, and ended up having to borrow a ticket to get past the ever alert gentleman at the bottom of the steps.

On a good day, these little foibles merely add to the character of Lord's, and I must admit happily that I normally get on very well with the great number of gatemen and doormen. It will always remain a shrine for the world's cricket lovers, whatever further changes lie in store, and is already the source of many of my favourite memories. The Australians are due back again this year, I wonder what is in store for them this time.

| England v Pakistan | 17th May - 21st May |
| England v Australia | 19th July - 23rd July |

1 Day NatWest series
England v Pakistan   12th June

The Final
Any combination of England,
Pakistan and Australia   23rd June

EVENT

*Lord's Cricket Ground
The Test Matches*

ADDRESS

*Lord's Cricket Ground
St Johns Wood Road
London
NW8 8QN*

EVENT DATE

See above for dates

WINNERS IN 2000

TICKETS & INFORMATION

020 7432 1066

*Sportsworld Hospitality Line
01235 555844*

WEB SITES

www.lords.org

For Hotel, Weather,
Travel Directions and
Additional Information
Visit
www.thesportingseason.com

The Vodafone *Derby*

PAUL HAYWARD - *Chief Sports Writer for The Daily Telegraph*

THE Derby is fighting back. The tumbleweeds are no longer blowing across Epsom Downs. In the early 1990s, the magic of Derby day evaporated, and the international racing calendar began to bulge with fresh multi-million dollar equine challenges. The world's greatest Flat race needed resuscitation, and fast.

"The Thoroughbred exists," wrote Federico Tesio, breeder of the great Ribot, "because its selection has depended not on experts, technicians or zoologists, but on a piece of wood; the winning post of the Epsom Derby." It was a clumsy sentence which expressed an eternal truth. The Derby doesn't revolve around the Thoroughbred. The Thoroughbred revolves around the Derby.

It was 1990 when the rot set in. On a dank, skin-chilling

afternoon, Quest For Fame ran across the depopulated Downs and into an emotional void. The Epsom roar had gone. A year later, when Generous's chestnut frame emerged from the pack rolling round Tattenham Corner, there were just 23,600 paying customers. Slowly, the organisers stirred. The unpromoted, mid-week, tradition-reliant national institution of old would have to get in a race of its own: to grab the attention of a sporting audience increasingly spoilt for choice.

The Derby is embedded in English consciousness. It is a hurdy-gurdy race staged on a funfair track surrounded by a human circus. Epsom on the first Wednesday in June always felt like being in a Dickens novel. Every social class sent representatives. The country sleepwalked on to the Downs. It was the race of Sea Bird and Nijinsky and Mill Reef and later Shergar, Nashwan

and Lammtarra. In this strange and often infuriating contest, Lester Piggott applied his strange brand of genius to the conquest of undulating and unforgiving Nature.

In the late Nineteenth Century, the Illustrated London News called Derby day, "the most astonishing, the most varied, the most picturesque and the most glorious spectacle that ever was, or ever can be, under any circumstances, visible to mortal eyes." The author plainly had a good lunch. But he was right in arguing that Derby Day was unmissable, not so much for the carousing and carousels as that agonising mile-and-a-half journey, which has never bestowed glory on a bad horse. Racing now imitates Formula One, with a world series of lucrative events across the globe. It made business sense

for it to be so, but the collateral damage to the Derby was substantial. For too long the event sold itself on prestige alone. When a slimy, gangly foal dropped into the hay, the owner always thought first of The Derby. The Epsom management are expending time and money to make breeders think that way again. Moving the race to Saturday afternoon was the first decisive act.

"In the early 1990s the day as an event was not being promoted," says Tim Darby, marketing manager at United Racecourses. "These days we play on the fact that it's worth £1m and is the supreme challenge for a three-year-old. When you've won The Derby you have a superstar horse. The event had lost its way in terms of being a national event. On Wednesday, it was competing with everything else that goes on in people's lives. We want it to have the same kind of buzz as the Grand

National, so that in the week before the race everybody's talking about who's going to win."

Purists would defend it to the last drop of blood. But then there were never enough purists to pack the Downs. Those of us who have an unbreakable love for The Derby would say that there is nothing to match the slam of the starting stalls down at the mile-and-a-half post, or the intestinal tightening which accompanies the helter-skelter ride towards Tattenham Corner, where the horses face a brutal test. Can they cope with the descent, the cambered straight, the noise-tunnel and the clatter of other hooves as the lungs begin to sting?

Whisper it in Louisville, but the Kentucky Derby is, by comparison, a mere scamper, a uniform and unvarying rush round a tight oval of flying dirt. Epsom on Derby day is where the Thoroughbred finds its raison d'etre.

EVENT

The Vodafone Derby

ADDRESS

The Grandstand
Epsom Downs
Surrey
KT18 5LQ

EVENT DATE

8th - 9th June 2001

WINNERS IN 2000

Sinndar
Ridden by Johnny Murtagh

TICKETS & INFORMATION

01372 470047

Sportsworld Hospitality Line
01235 555844

WEB SITES

www.epsomderby.co.uk

For Hotel, Weather,
Travel Directions and
Additional Information
Visit
www.thesportingseason.com

The *Stella Artois*
Championships Queen's Club

ROGER TAYLOR - *former Wimbledon Semi-finalist and Davis Cup Captain*

The Stella Artois Championships, held at the Queen's Club in London's fashionable West Kensington area, is the first major grass court tournament of the season in England starting with the Stella and finishing on the centre court at Wimbledon. It's a fascinating date in the grass court season when the top players rent houses in the West Kensington and Wimbledon area in order to settle into Britain and hone their game to the grass after a gruelling clay court season. They now need vital grass court practice to prepare themselves mentally and physically for Wimbledon.

The venue at Queen's has always attracted a strong field of contenders. Top players like Sampras, McEnroe, Becker and Edberg have all won Queen's and then gone on to become Wimbledon Champion, many players choose to play doubles as well as singles to gain that invaluable extra grass court practice. Usually a huge serve combined with lightning reflexes and the ability to move forward to volley helps a player; the points are quick, so good concentration is also necessary to be a success on grass. Whereas, to be a great clay court player you need to be able to run all day with the stamina of an ox and you must never miss a ball just to be able to survive.

Traditionally the players with a classic serve and volley game were the ones winning titles on the lawns of England. Great Champions like Sampras, Borg, McEnroe, Becker, Edberg all fit the mould of grass court champions. Many of the new up and coming players favour the baseline, hitting big heavy topspin ground strokes. Lleyton Hewitt, defending Stella Artois Champion is a good example. This style of play has become necessary as the majority of tournaments are now played on slow to medium paced courts. Players to watch out for now are Gustavo Kuerten from Brazil and 2000 French Open Champion, Lleyton Hewitt, Marit Safin an all court player from Russia who blew Sampras away in straight sets to win the 2000 US Open, and Roger Federer from Switzerland. Nowadays this new breed of player, both men and women, combine their skills to win on all surfaces. I personally don't think it will be long before we see an unforgettable final at Wimbledon or the Stella, played almost entirely from the baseline.

Britain hopes that Tim Henman or Greg Rusedski can win Wimbledon this year. Both have the big serve and volley game, which does put them in the elite group who can win! In 1998 Tim Henman was runner up to Pete Sampras in the Stella Artois final and lost out to Sampras again in the Wimbledon semi-final that same year. He had a great 2000 and is still improving. Greg Rusedski struggled to find his best form last year, injuries haven't helped, but he can turn it all around very quickly once he gets his game back on track. Looking elsewhere, Martin Lee, Jamie Delgado, Barry Cowan and Arvind Palmer are all looking to break into the top one hundred this year and eighteen year old Lee Childs is progressing well, however, he has three hard years ahead of him before he really arrives on the scene.

In the next five or so years it is possible for a Brit to win Wimbledon, but for this year my favourite will be Pete Sampras. It's hard to see him being beaten if he's on form, after seven titles he's probably the greatest grass court player ever, but you never know......?

EVENT

The Stella Artois Championships Queen's Club

ADDRESS

Queen's Club Palliser Road West Kensington W14 9EQ

EVENT DATE

11th - 17th June 2001

WINNERS IN 2000

Lleyton Hewitt

TICKETS & INFORMATION

020 7413 1444

Sportsworld Hospitality Line 01235 555844

WEB SITES

For Hotel, Weather, Travel Directions and Additional Information Visit www.thesportingseason.com

A conference in Mexico,
hospitality at Wimbledon,
or an incentive package to the Olympics

Sportsworld – a world of experience

We have the experience and logistical expertise to ensure the smooth running of all kinds of corporate events – worldwide. Over the last 20 years the Sportsworld Group has developed into a total corporate resource, serving organising committees and corporate clients. Our meticulous levels of planning and highly focused staff enable us to provide an uncompomising level of customer satisfaction. **It's official** - we pride ourselves on exclusive supply of officially sanctioned tickets and programmes and have been the Official Ticket and Tour Operator for many world leading sporting events including 5 FIFA World Cups and the recent 'best ever' Olympic Games in Sydney.

Whatever your event entails; be it a champagne theatre evening in London's West End, a day's hospitality at Wimbledon or a 10,000 delegate congress on the other side of the world, it will be our pleasure to make it a success.

SPORTSWORLD
a world of experience

www.sportsworld-group.plc.uk

SPORTSWORLD TRAVEL • SPORTSWORLD HOSPITALITY • SHOW WORLD • CONGRESS WORLD • MARTLET
TEL: 01235 555 844   FAX: 01235 550 428   E-MAIL: hospitality@sportsworld-group.plc.uk

ABINGDON • BRIGHTON • LONDON • ATLANTA • AUCKLAND • CALGARY • KUALA LUMPUR • JOHANNESBURG • MEXICO CITY • SYDNEY

Royal *Ascot*

HARRY HERBERT - *Managing Director of Highclere Thoroughbred Racing*

There can be few more intoxicating sporting events in the world than the four days in June that make up the Royal Meeting at Ascot. It must also surely be one of the most extraordinary sights in world sport which sees Europe's most talented equine athletes competing before a crowd of over fifty thousand beautifully dressed spectators - the men in top hat and tails and the ladies donning the finest fashions. You simply cannot fail but to be deeply impressed by the sheer spectacle, whether you are a keen race-goer, or just there to soak up the sights.

The action starts shortly after two o'clock each day when Her Majesty The Queen arrives with the Royal party in open landau carriages – in itself, a marvellous spectacle. The procession makes its way from the top of the straight down past the grandstands and then passes in front of a sea of photographers, who are eager not only to photograph Her Majesty but also the bevy of beauties and international stars who are only too keen to show off their new hats and frocks.

The racing is the best in the world and on each of the four days includes at least one Group One event (the crème de la crème). There is definitely no such thing as a bad race, which is why it is every owner's dream to stand on the hallowed turf of the winners enclosure. I was lucky enough to realise this dream in 1997 when one of Highclere's horses, Heritage, won the King George V Handicap - a victory which will remain indelibly imprinted in the minds of everyone involved. So excited were my owners, that Frankie Dettori executed one of his famous flying dismounts (see photograph), something he only normally performs after a Classic or principal Group race win.

From a racing point of view, there really is something for everyone. The Kings Stand Stakes, at one end of the scale is run over five furlongs in approximately a minute whilst at the other end, there is the Ascot Gold Cup over two and a half miles which takes over four minutes to run. There are also some of the most competitive handicaps in the racing calendar, including the Royal Hunt Cup and the Wokingham, which often attract fields of some thirty runners. If you manage to pick the winner of one of these two races, you will almost certainly be walking away having beaten the bookies – something that I have so far failed to achieve in goodness knows how many years of attending the meeting.

The two most prestigious two-year-old races are the Coventry Stakes for colts, which is run over six furlongs on the first day of the meeting, and the Queen Mary Stakes for fillies, which is run over

the minimum trip of five furlongs on the Wednesday. These are two races that throughout the winter every owner in the land dreams of winning with one of their unraced babies – a dream which probably gives credence to the belief that no owner of an unraced two-year-old ever commits suicide!

Apart from Heritage giving us our first Royal Ascot winner, my happiest memories revolve around two horses that my father owned called Little Wolf and Lyric Fantasy. The former won the Ascot Gold Cup in great style back in 1983 and this is one of only a couple of races where Her Majesty actually makes an official

presentation to the owner within the Royal Box. Lyric Fantasy, a tiny filly standing only fourteen hands three inches high, was bought for 13,000 Guineas but turned out to be one of the fastest two-year-olds seen since the War. In 1992, she came to the Queen Mary, having impressively won her first two starts; Richard Hannon, her trainer, had publicly stated that she was, without doubt, the fastest two-year-old that he had ever trained. He also described her to the press as having the face of a model and the backside of a scullery maid! In the Queen Mary, she literally blitzed her opposition showing a devastating display of sustained speed. She won by five lengths and became the first two-year-old to run this trip at Ascot in under a minute - an extraordinary record which still stands today.

Whilst Royal Ascot is partly about pageantry, style and glamour, it is primarily and most importantly about watching the best Thoroughbreds in the world competing against one another. There is, quite simply, no other sporting event in the world like it.

EVENT

Royal Ascot

ADDRESS

Ascot Racecourse
Ascot
Berkshire
SL5 7JN

EVENT DATE

19th - 22nd June 2001

WINNERS IN 2000

Kayf-tara
ridden by Mick Kinane
(The Gold Cup)

TICKETS & INFORMATION

01344 876876

Sportsworld Hospitality Line
01235 555844

WEB SITES

www.ascot.co.uk

For Hotel, Weather,
Travel Directions and
Additional Information
Visit
www.thesportingseason.com

IMAGINATION *by*

Catherine Best

THE MILL, STEAM MILL LANE,
ST. MARTIN'S, GUERNSEY GY4 6XE
TEL: +44 (0)1481 237771
WEBSITE: www.catherinebest.com

The Championships
Wimbledon

VIRGINIA WADE - *Wimbledon Singles Champion & BBC Commentator*

E ach year there is no change. The trophy is a beautiful gold cup. The hands that clasp it and the lips that kiss it are the same it seems as every prior year. They belong to Pete Sampras who virtually owns the trophy this decade. At the beginning of July every year since 1992, with one exception, he has won it. The name Pete Sampras and the Wimbledon men's singles are synonymous.

It sounds pretty old hat, as if it is just more of the same, by definition, boring and staid. It might suggest that The Championships is stuck in a rut, but on the contrary, winning Wimbledon can never get monotonous.... the more repeat wins, the more dramatically exciting.

Wimbledon itself never gets mundane. It's prestige just keeps growing and growing. If it works, don't fix it! The trick is to re-invent itself each year as if it's brand new, but simultaneously is the same perfect, old traditional, ancestral family home. It's required to have the comfort and wisdom of a grandfather along with the spark of an energetic teenager.

Four years ago when the new No.1 court opened, I had been hitting at the practice courts at Aorangi before the tournament started. As I played with the new stadium as a backdrop, I thought to myself, "Wimbledon will never be the same for me again. The original and familiar No.1 court has been razed to the ground, the vista of the back

courts and the centre court has been taken away, and instead this huge concrete stadium has been erected." Well, I felt like that for about two days. Then shortly after, there was the emotional opening ceremony. Inside, the arena was gorgeous, formed perfectly in the image of its venerable parent, the Centre Court. I grew fond of the look, even from the back. In fact it is one of the pleasures of being at Wimbledon, to wander up to the high ground at the back where the purple petunias not only perfume the air, but, adjacent to the green grass, decorate the scene with the club colours.

The new No.1 court was just the beginning of the improvements. No sooner was it completed than work started on the construction of the new Millennium Building, which had its grand opening at last year's tournament. It's a spectacular place for the privileged members and players to relax and mingle in their respective areas. The players have their own protected private entrance, so that they can arrive with their entourages and not be scrutinised by the public. The latter still stand patiently outside the main entrance hoping for a sighting of someone famous attending the royal box, but their close view of the players coming and going has gone. Alas, they cannot even sight the competitors on their long walk to their match courts, as the contenders can scurry to and fro in an underground tunnel. The public may have to sacrifice some of the old Wimbledon's intimacy, but the players have gained in the process.

As a player, one has the most enviable bird's eye view of the panorama of the front courts from the upper floors of the competitors restaurant. One can relax there if it's not too cold, spectate and even eat at the same time. When there is still time to spare, there is always the state of the art gym, in which to work out and fine tune a few more muscles to elevate one's game. Or if that is not one's fancy, there are computers to access e-mail, or

63

perhaps check out one's popularity on a personal website!

So ultra modern is Wimbledon today and yet so traditional.

The committee retains the right to make decisions peculiar to the Championships, such as seedings which defy the players' associations ranking lists. They insist on rewarding the men with higher prize money, despite the fact that supposedly we live in a world of equal opportunity in the 21st century. The incredible numbers that viewed the men's final last year on TV, which the long rain delay sent into prime time on Sunday evening, defended the committee's theory. But by the same token, one should pay attention to the extraordinary numbers that turned up in person, or watched on TV, the

postponed ladies' doubles final between the new
Wimbledon ladies' champion, Venus Williams, and her
equally magnetic sister. The match was delayed till the
third Monday of the tournament when the Millennium
Championships ended with a flourish during that small
window of dry weather. Once again Wimbledon fulfilled
its role as the showcase of the tennis world. Not only did
it enthral the public with phenomenal tennis played on
perfect grass courts, but also it ushered in the new
century with a promise of more of the same yet
something new. One can never dispute the fact that a
day at Wimbledon is like winning the lottery - which in
reality is the only way, a regular member of the public
can get there!

EVENT

The Championships
Wimbledon

ADDRESS

The All England Club
Church Road
Wimbledon
London
SW19 5AE

EVENT DATE

25th June - 8th July 2001
(not Sunday 1st July)

WINNERS IN 2000

Pete Sampras
Venus Williams

TICKETS & INFORMATION

020 8971 2473

Sportsworld Hospitality Line
01235 555844

WEB SITES

www.wimbledon.org

For Hotel, Weather,
Travel Directions and
Additional Information
Visit
www.thesportingseason.com

MATCH POINT

OPENING SERVICE

WIMBLEDON TENNIS CHAMPIONSHIPS	25 June - 8 July
BOODLE & DUNTHORNE LEGENDS TENNIS CLASSIC, MOTTRAM HALL	26 June - 29 July
VEUVE CLICQUOT GOLD CUP POLO, COWDRAY PARK	30 June - 22 July
HAMPTON COURT PALACE INTERNATIONAL FLOWER SHOW	3 - 8 July
HENLEY ROYAL REGATTA	4 - 8 July
1ST TEST MATCH, ENGLAND V AUSTRALIA, EDGBASTON	5 - 9 July
GLORIOUS GOODWOOD	31 July - 4 August
COWES WEEK	4 - 11 August

Veuve Clicquot

CHAMPAGNE OF THE SEASON

Henley
Royal Regatta

SIR STEVEN REDGRAVE - *Five Times Olympic Gold Medallist*

The most prestigious event in the rowing calendar each year is without doubt "The Henley Royal Regatta", attracting people from all walks of life, some to enjoy the social whirl of high society sipping champagne or Pimms, others to make a dream come true and race on the world famous Henley course.

Henley Town could be described as schizoid for it exhibits a split personality. During the winter months it is a peaceful, rural town in which traffic jams are seldom found and the river at its best is uninviting. By April the character transformation has begun with the erection of numerous marquees on the river banks and the delineation of the course on the river itself. The hype increases in early June when overseas crews arrive to prepare for the big event. For seven brief days at the beginning of July each year Henley becomes the high spot for high society, it boasts traffic jams worse than the city of London, the biggest picnic in Europe and thousands of young debutantes parade in the latest fashions as though on a catwalk. Within days of the finish of racing the hubbub dies, Henley is thrown back into tranquillity and virtual oblivion for yet another year.

But what of the racing – for after all without rowing this spectacle would be no spectacle at all. The inaugural regatta took place in 1839 when there were only two events. The Town Challenge Cup in which any male crew of four oarsmen was eligible to race so long as they all lived within a five mile radius of Henley, and the Grand Challenge Cup a race for eights.

Royal patronage was not granted until 1851 when Prince Albert contributed £50 to the regatta's then ailing finances. Today, 150 years later, the Town Challenge Cup is no longer raced for in this regatta, but the Grand Challenge Cup is still contested. The "Grand", as it is referred to, is a race for eights open to any rowing club in the world. It is looked upon by many as the blue ribboned event of the regatta, the final of the "Grand" may be watched each year at 3 p.m. on the 1st day of racing.

In addition to the "Grand", there are thirteen other events providing racing for a wide spectrum of boat categories. The rules of racing state that crews must qualify at preliminary regattas or in the qualifying races held in the week before the main regatta.

The course runs from the Berkshire side of Temple Island, one and a quarter miles upstream, and is clearly marked by booms which minimise the wash of other river traffic and provide a clear channel for racing. Crews race side by side in a head to head contest, the winner going through to the next days racing, the loser retiring gracefully to the beer tent!

HENLEY
ROYAL
REGATTA
STEWARDS'
ENCLOSURE
GUEST

SUNDAY
July 4th, 1999

DS 2635

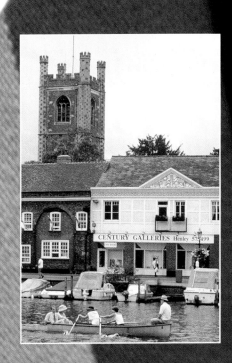

EVENT

Henley Royal
Regatta

ADDRESS

Regatta Headquarters
Henley - on - Thames
Oxfordshire
RG9 2LY

EVENT DATE

4th - 8th July 2001

WINNERS IN 2000

The Australian Institute
of Sport (The Grand)

TICKETS & INFORMATION

01491 572153

Sportsworld Hospitality Line
01235 555844

WEB SITES

www.hrr.co.uk

For Hotel, Weather,
Travel Directions and
Additional Information
Visit
www.thesportingseason.com

Perhaps the most unusual aspect of racing at Henley is the fact that a good club crew could be drawn to race against the reigning world champions, an opportunity that other regattas in England are not able to offer!

Any onlooker to the spectacle of the regatta would wonder what attracts crews from all over the world to the Henley course, for indeed it has to be said that it is the ambition of all active oarsmen, to compete at Henley.

I, personally, think it is the magical atmosphere that exists at Henley during the regatta which attracts competitors. It is the only time that a rower comes close to competing in the buzz of a packed stadium.

Until very recently, this highly successful rowing extravaganza played no part in the development of the National Rowing Team. The regatta was merely a show piece for all interested parties. As of a few years ago, however, the regatta committee decided to contribute a sum of money each year to the Junior National Rowing Team. It was felt by all concerned that by supporting the Junior Team, the regatta was indirectly supporting the Senior Team of the future and, of course, in essence this is true.

100 SPORTS ON ONE FLOOR. TRY THEM ALL.

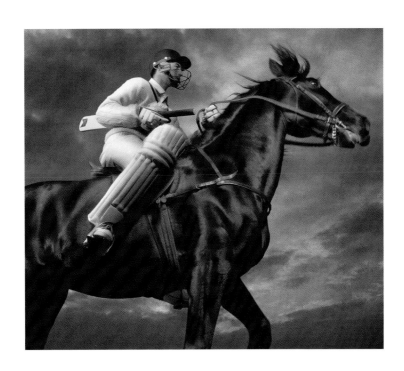

THE NEW EXPANDED SPORTS FLOOR.
OPENING TIMES: MONDAY TO SATURDAY, 10AM TO 7PM.

Sports, Fifth Floor, Harrods Ltd., Knightsbridge, London SW1X 7XL.
Telephone 020 7730 1234. www.harrods.com

The Fosters *British Formula One* Grand Prix

NIGEL MANSELL - *Former World Champion*

I might have won my first grand prix at Brands Hatch but Silverstone ran through my career like a golden thread. In many ways, it all started there for me when I did what I call my first mega-test for Lotus in 1980. This led to me getting that coveted initial drive in Formula One and from here the work began in earnest. There weren't many people watching that day but later they would come in they're hundreds of thousands. There was nowhere like the old Silverstone. It was unique. It still gives me the chills thinking about driving down the Hangar Straight on qualifying tyres and taking Stowe flat out at about 200mph. Then there was the short shoot to Club corner and trying to take that pretty much flat out, too. Abbey was totally flat, Woodcote was close and there was that special sequence of corners around Beckets.

There is some wonderful, marvellous history attached to the place. Some great deeds in motor racing have been done there on that old windswept airfield. It saddens me that it has been chopped up recently because I think that has stifled a lot of the excitement for the drivers and for the supporters but I know the authorities did it with the best of intentions. It's not the same now, though.

One of my best memories is 1987 when I had that duel with Nelson Piquet. The highlight was me doing a dummy on him coming up the Hangar Straight. A lot of people still talk about that move and it's on quite a few highlights videos. It gave me a tremendous amount of satisfaction at the time and that was my first British Grand Prix win at Silverstone. The year after that, there was that very dramatic race in the rain.

What I will always remember most about Silverstone, though, are the crowds. They were magnificent to me there every year. It just made it into a sensational experience, the flags, the cheering, and the wall of sound. It gave me a real lift every year. Perhaps it's not the same for some other drivers, but it gave me such a boost, the atmosphere somehow inspired me to drive quicker than ever at Silverstone.

I won there again in 1991 and 1992. In qualifying for the race in 1992, I was about two seconds quicker than anybody else was. I remember Riccardo Patrese, my Williams team-mate, coming up to me at the end of that session and telling me in a particular way that he could not believe how I had summoned the nerve to set the time that I had. He said he didn't know where all that extra time had come from. That was a nice moment.

Winning the race that year was special, too. It was my World Championship year and the support was incredible. It was one of the most magical and emotional weekends of my entire life. From first practice on Friday to the chequered flag on Sunday none of the other cars mattered. When I took that chequered flag at the end, it was total mayhem. There were people all over the track, wanting to congratulate me. I ran over some bloke's foot but he didn't seem too worried about it. There was just a feeling of joy and celebration everywhere that was fantastic to be a part of.

Two laps before the end of the race, I put in a really fast lap and lowered the track record by two seconds. I didn't do that for my benefit, I did it for the fans because they deserved it. It was my little present to them to thank them for their loyalty. I wanted it to be my tribute to them.

It's a shame there has been so much controversy surrounding the staging of the race at the circuit in recent years. I was part of the television team there last season and the galling thing about the situation was that it seemed it would take so little to fix it. It was just a matter of common-sense and spending a little bit of money.

I believe with careful planning and more hard-standing car parking the facilities would be extremely good. It's disappointing that the weather gets blamed for everything that goes wrong in sport in this country. Somewhere along the line, we have got to wise up because there is always a chance that the weather is going to be bad and that should not be an excuse any longer.

Surely, we have got the wherewithal to cope with a bit of rain. I know that Silverstone has been awarded the race on a long-term basis now and hopefully that is an indication that lessons have been learned. It is a great old circuit and it deserves better than to have its reputation sullied by a few problems that can be easily rectified.

EVENT

The Fosters
British Formula 1
Grand Prix

ADDRESS

Silverstone Circuit
Silverstone
Towcester
Northamptonshire
NN12 8TN

EVENT DATE

13th - 15th July 2001

WINNERS IN 2000

David Coulthard

TICKETS & INFORMATION

01327 850202

Sportsworld Hospitality Line
01235 555844

WEB SITES

www.silverstone-circuit.co.uk

For Hotel, Weather,
Travel Directions and
Additional Information
Visit
www.thesportingseason.com

The Open Championship

NICK FALDO - *Five Times Major Winner*

The atmosphere of the Open is different to that of any other major Championship. Only the Masters comes close and that is probably because it has one home, Augusta National. I played a few holes around St Andrews on the Sunday before the Championship last year, the huge grandstands were empty and there was something very eerie about it. Even the ball sounds different. Links courses by nature are difficult to pin down but stands mark them out so well. They give them a definition. It was blowing a gale and I had a nice feeling going back to St Andrews. When I played the 18th in practice I could visualise what the scene would be like on the final day. The stands would not be empty. There would be 10,000 voices.

The first time I won the Open was at Muirfield in 1987. I remember talking to myself before the Championship started, I was saying "I'm 30 years of age and if you're going to do it, now is the time and now is the place".

Nineteen of the Top 20 Americans were there. We had the world's best field and that inspired me. I thought to myself that if I'm going to win let's beat everybody. Mentally, I felt strong and my game was good. I walked out of the exhibition tent and looked at the empty leaderboard. I visualised my name at the top. I walked another ten steps and suddenly felt very comfortable with that thought..... my name will be at the top of the leaderboard at the end of the week. It was a strange feeling. I knew exactly what would happen.

On the final day I shot an unbelievable round of golf. Nobody can expect to shoot 18 straight pars to win the Open, for it to happen like that was quite amazing. Over the back nine holes I felt total pressure .... my first chance to win a major. The weather was awful and the course was playing so long. It was like playing in pea soup. One bad mistake could have blown everything.

In those conditions pars were good scores. I just told myself to keep it going, keep hitting the shots. Making par after par was not my game plan but I was happy to settle for it. I made three important saves and the pressure was building more and more. I was one shot behind Paul Azinger going into the final round and he continued to defy logic because he had never seen a links course before arriving at Muirfield. On the final day he continued to bowl along and he went to the turn in 34. I could do nothing but make pars although I was within inches of birdies at each of the first five holes.

On three occasions in four holes from the seventh I got up and down from bunkers to save pars. Azinger had gone three shots clear but when he dropped strokes at the 10th and the 11th he came under pressure and I was determined not to do anything reckless. At the 18th, one of my lasting memories is of my 5 iron to the green. I knew that when the ball landed on the green I had done everything humanly possible. I was at five under for the Championship and I still had to make a four and a half footer for par and a round of 71. I thought that if I missed it I was not going to win the Open. Just get the blooming thing in the hole!

Then I waited. I sat in the R & A caravan, a TV set on the right, a TV set on the left. I almost had my head between my knees. My daughter, Natalie who was

born the year before, kept pressing the TV buttons. I remember thinking I've still got to be mentally ready, in case of a play off. When Azinger was on the 18th green, Peter Alliss said the next 15 seconds was going to change either my life or Azinger's. Looking back, the round I played was one of which Jack Nicklaus would have been proud.

When I returned to Muirfield in 1992, I was a different person and the circumstances were so different. I was the favourite and I was playing and hitting the ball so well. I was four shots in the lead going into the final round and if I hadn't won it would have been disastrous. Things did go wrong in the last round but I couldn't face losing it. This was my Open. I had done all the work throughout the week and I had led for a long time. All of a sudden John Cook had taken over and once again the 18th was a key hole. It is such a tough finishing hole.

The 18th was a great test of my technique. This time it was down to sheer guts and willpower. I had one more chance and I just could not give it away. My 3 iron approach at the flag was as memorable as the 5 iron five years earlier. I'm quite proud of both shots. When I won by a stroke I'd never felt quite so.... it was almost shock. I felt hungry, sick – everything was emotional. As you say to yourself "you've won" your mind switches off and there is a massive drop. Everything comes out and there is a huge rush of adrenalin.

St Andrew's in 1990 was very different from Muifield. I'd won the Masters and just missed the US Open and I was determined to win the Open. I was in total control, I played great, putted great and when you put the two together............ Any opportunity I had I knocked it in. I believed I could get round in 67 and I was doing it. I've never putted better. I never missed a birdie chance and all the long putts went close. I made a few easy mistakes and never put myself under pressure. It was a dream.

My worst experience in an Open was at Royal St George's in 1985, the year Sandy Lyle won. I was at home by the time Sandy won. I had committed myself to a swing change under David Leadbetter and it was just the beginning. It wasn't me at Sandwich. I wasn't doing anything right. That was the start of my early dark days.

I had a terrible time and it was a hard week to take. It really knocked me. Apart from anything else my putting was so bad. I went to Sunningdale to try out a number of putters with my friend, Mark Wildey. He's a left hander and he beat me putting right-handed. To me the hole was the size of a thimble and it had cling film on top.

The majors, of course, are my main goal. I have three Opens and two Masters and although I'm not chasing records there is still more work to do. I don't think of the glory bit. I just feel I want to do more. I would like to think I've got 10 more good years.

EVENT

The Open
Championship

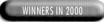

ADDRESS

Royal Lytham &
St Annes Golf Course
Links Gate
Lytham St. Anne
Lancashire FY8 3LQ

EVENT DATE

19th - 22nd July 2001

WINNERS IN 2000

Tiger Woods

TICKETS & INFORMATION

01334 478478

Sportsworld Hospitality Line
01235 555844

WEB SITES

www.opengolf.com

For Hotel, Weather,
Travel Directions and
Additional Information
Visit
www.thesportingseason.com

Every year
one child in
thirty is born
with a disability
that may affect
them for life.
SPARKS mission
is to help babies to
be born healthy and
to stay healthy.

SPARKS, 10 Dean Farrar Street, London, SW1H 0DX Tel 020 7799 2111 Fax 020 7222 2701

www.sparks.org.uk

Registered Charity No. 1003825

Cartier
International *Polo*

LORD BERESFORD - *Former England International*

The annual show-piece of British polo takes place on the last Sunday in July, in Windsor Great Park. It is widely known as "Cartier Day", in recognition of its long and ongoing sponsorship by the famous Bond Street jewellers.

"Cartier Day" provides all that is best and most glamorous in the sport – top players, superb ponies, huge crowds, massive hospitality, intense excitement. And because the venue is The Guards Polo Club, Her Majesty The Queen is invariably present, as well as marching bands from the Brigade of Guards, plus celebrities galore from the world of show business and fashion.

Always there are two matches, both of which used to be played in the afternoon. Nowadays the format has changed: the first starts at 11am, followed by a suitably lengthy break for lunch, then the second – the Coronation Cup – at 3.30pm.

Formerly the supporting game was known as the "Silver Jubilee Cup" and always featured The Prince of Wales, but because he no longer plays competitively, it has become the "Prince Philip Trophy", and pits the winners of the British Open – the Cowdray Gold Cup – against a team composed of four of the best young English players. A contest of nail-biting tension invariably ensues.

The Coronation Cup itself was first presented in 1911 to commemorate the coronation of King George V. As befitted a period when the sun never set on the British Empire, it is of a size and grandeur that is amazing to behold. The intention was that it should be the "Champion of Champions' Cup" i.e. that it should be decided between the winners of the four London Open Tournaments – the Hurlingham, Ranelagh and Roehampton Opens and the Inter-Regimental, plus any approved teams representing India or other colonies and dominions of the Empire. Thus it remained until 1939, with the exception of the years 1914-1918, when no major polo took place in this country due to the First World War, and in which incidentally many of our finest

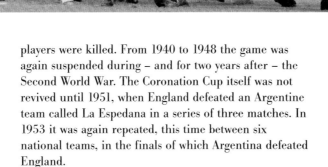

players were killed. From 1940 to 1948 the game was again suspended during – and for two years after – the Second World War. The Coronation Cup itself was not revived until 1951, when England defeated an Argentine team called La Espedana in a series of three matches. In 1953 it was again repeated, this time between six national teams, in the finals of which Argentina defeated England.

Thereafter it lapsed, languishing for 17 years in the vaults of the Hurlingham Polo Association's bank, until in 1971 it became the prize for an annual contest between England and the United States. Initially the game took place at Cowdray, but from 1972 onwards at Windsor, where it blossomed into the great fiesta of polo we see today, incorporating after 1974 not just the United States but a variety of other opponents for England including Argentina, Australasia, Brazil, Chile, France, Mexico, New Zealand, South Africa, Spain etc. Many great games have resulted, and curiously, in view of our notorious climate, it has never had to be cancelled on account of the weather.

EVENT

Cartier
International Polo

ADDRESS

Guards Polo Club
Smiths Lawn
Windsor Great Park
Egham
TW20 0HP

EVENT DATE

29th July 2001

WINNERS IN 2000

Argentina

TICKETS & INFORMATION

01784 437797 from April

Sportsworld Hospitality Line
01235 555844

WEB SITES

www.guardspoloclub.com

For Hotel, Weather,
Travel Directions and
Additional Information
Visit
www.thesportingseason.com

Altogether there are invariably more than 20,000 spectators. Some are "afficionadas", some have never witnessed polo before. Many bring a picnic, whilst others head for the hospitality tents. In the Cartier marquee alone over 700 guests sit down to enjoy a lunch prepared by Anton Mosimann, long regarded as one of the world's greatest chefs, amidst decoration inspired by Kelly Hoppen, another leader in her field. The party is hosted by Cartier's Managing Director Arnaud Bamberger and his lovely wife Carla, with the help of their supremely elegant Communications Director Pilar Boxford.

So great has been the success of "Cartier Day" that is has become by far the greatest fund raiser for the Hurlingham Polo Association, all profits being ploughed back into the sport, to the benefit of every single Club in the country, and particularly to the advantage of promising young players from schools, universities and the Pony Club.

It is truly a day to remember.

Tank Française Watch - www.cartier.com

Glorious *Goodwood*

(The July Festival Meeting)

THE EARL OF MARCH - *Guardian of the Goodwood Estate*

'Glorious Goodwood' – the alliterative epithet trips easily off the tongue, but it also rings absolutely true. The setting of Goodwood racecourse, perched on top of the South Downs is incomparable with its views over rolling downland to the north and the coastal plain, Chichester Cathedral and, on a clear day, the Isle of Wight to the south and south-west.

Those views, particularly to the north where it takes an eagle eye to discern a single building in the folds of the Downs, have changed little since Wednesday April 28th 1802, when the first Goodwood race meeting opened and extended over three days, with the 3rd Duke of Richmond appropriately winning a Sweepstakes with Cedar and a Hunters' Plate with You-Know-Me.

Ten years later, on May 4th 1812, the Goodwood Cup, then called simply 'The Gold Cup', was run for the first time. It was to become the centrepiece of the whole Goodwood racing programme, and retains its prestige as one of the supreme tests of stamina on the British Turf right down to the present day, having been won by such immortals as Kinscem, St Simon, Brown Jack, Alycidon and, in the 1990s, Further Flight and Double Trigger.

In the course of time, the Goodwood meeting shifted from April-May, when the top of the Downs can be chilly and windswept, to late July, when the weather is more likely to match the glory of its situation. The July meeting was the only meeting until after the First World War, but then fuller use began to be made of the unique course and its magnificent facilities. By the time the millennium was reached, Goodwood was host to twenty days racing a year, beginning with a three-day meeting in May and including four evening meetings in June, five days at the July or Festival meeting, further meetings in late August and early September and concluding with a two-day meeting in late September.

The majority of the prestigious and best-endowed races are run at the July meeting. They include the ever-popular J P Morgan Goodwood Cup and the Vodafone Stewards' Cup, first run in 1840 and one of the most competitive sprint handicaps in the calendar, providing a cavalry charge of thirty runners up the straight six furlongs. They are supplemented by the Champagne

Lanson Sussex Stakes and the Vodafone Nassau Stakes, both enjoying Group 1 status which places them among the twenty-seven most important races run throughout the UK. Both races have long histories; the Vodafone Nassau Stakes having been founded the same year as the Vodafone Stewards' Cup and the Champagne Lanson Sussex Stakes a year later. Their high status was underlined in 2000 by the victories of that horse of steel, Giant's Causeway, the winner of five Group 1 races altogether, in the Champagne Lanson Sussex Stakes, and of that admirable filly, Crimplene, the winner of Classic races in Germany and Ireland, in the Vodafone Nassau Stakes.

Two men stand out as contributors to Goodwood's reputation as a racecourse and to its special flavour in the social world – Lord George Bentinck and King Edward VII. Bentinck, for many years a close friend of the fourth Duke of Richmond, was a great administrator and innovator who, in the 1830s reconstructed the course and made it the fine and fair test of the racehorse which we know today; whilst Edward VII, first as Prince of Wales and later as King, was a regular guest for the annual race meetings and gave attendance at Goodwood meetings a permanent social cachet enhanced by the stand-rebuilding programme of the last thirty years including the major development opening on July 31st, which has given the course amenities to rival the best in the country.

EVENT

Glorious Goodwood
The July Festival
Meeting

ADDRESS

Goodwood Racecourse
Goodwood
Chichester
West Sussex
PO18 0PS

EVENT DATE

31st July - 4th August 2001

WINNERS IN 2000

Giant's Causeway ridden by
Mick Kinane (The Champagne
Lanson Sussex Stakes)

TICKETS & INFORMATION

0800 0188191

Sportsworld Hospitality Line
01235 555844

WEB SITES

www.goodwood.co.uk

For Hotel, Weather,
Travel Directions and
Additional Information
Visit
www.thesportingseason.com

Skandia Life
Cowes Week

LAWRIE SMITH - *Olympic Medallist & Around the World Yachtsman*

Cowes Week, the annual waterside jamboree centred at the heart of British yachting in Cowes on the Isle of Wight, blends all that is quintessentially English about yacht racing.

For the first week in August – the date is set by the first Saturday always following the last Tuesday in July – Royalty and their commoners rub shoulders afloat, if not ashore, levelled for once by the capricious winds and waters of The Solent – the stretch of water between mainland England and the Isle of Wight – which respect neither class nor wealth. Cowes comes alive, imbued with the spirit of its biggest week of the year and decorated in flags, banners and more recently prominent sponsor's regalia. In recent years sponsors like Land Rover and the insurance company Skandia Life have supported the Cowes Combined Clubs in their organisation of the event.

Cowes Week is a week of very serious light-hearted sailing that began sometime in the early 1800s and which then, as now, was attended and participated in

enthusiastically by generations of the British Royal family and their Royal friends and relations from abroad, as well as the landed gentry and working sailors.

The week was a particular favourite of the Duke of Edinburgh who, until recently, had been racing nearly every year for 30 years. More recently his son, Prince Edward, has taken to sailing, sharing steering duties with Prince Constantine of Greece, usually aboard the Yeoman yachts owned by the Aisher family of Marley Tile fame.

In 1957 overseas entries to Cowes Week were encouraged by the inauguration of the Admiral's Cup for three-boat national teams. That year just two teams, Britain and America, contested a friendly and decidedly low-key regatta, victory resting with the home team. Today 43 years later, the Champagne Mumm Admirals Cup, as it is now known, is held a few weeks before Cowes Week, but it is still recognised as the unofficial world championship of offshore racing.

The Admiral's Cup was recently split from the main thrust of Cowes Week racing itself, its international competitors seeking open and uninterrupted waters to more evenly conduct their battles, but its influence has changed Cowes Week forever.

Today teams of surveyors, corporate business clients, friends from the country and casual sailors collectively, somewhat unkindly, known as

DFTs (Down from Towns) by the professionals take Cowes Week and its prestigious trophies – the New York Yacht Club Challenge Cup and the Britannia Cup – relatively seriously. Well, with a boat costing anything up to £0.5 million you would, wouldn't you?

But for me Cowes Week has often meant work. The work of yacht racing is my chosen career. Despite the image of fun, sea and sun, the business of yacht racing is as serious as any city dealer's. Races, particularly Cowes Week races, are not won by luck alone, although that can be useful. Preparation of the boat and the crew and a thorough knowledge of the local idiosyncrasies and expected weather conditions are as essential to me as the Tokyo closing prices or the predictions for opening in New York.

Work for me in Cowes has usually meant the Admiral's Cup. I've sailed for Britain six times and was immensely proud to skipper the top boat in the series, Jamarella, in 1989 as part of a winning British team. The bars are places to infiltrate the opposition for tactical titbits or

snippets of weather information as well as trying to elicit information on their boats' performances.

But when the owners and socialites head for the exclusive balls of the Royal Yacht Squadron where the Duke of Edinburgh is Admiral – or the Royal London or Royal Corinthian Yacht Clubs where lesser gentry reside, I tend to join my sailing colleagues in our team headquarters for an early night far from the madding crowd which can be heard at play all over town.

Cowes Week is all things to all men: Formula One cars and Stock Cars on the same track, royalty and commoners at the same dances. It is a week of frenzied hedonism at every imaginable level: late-night whirling for 'the social set', a tough sail and a rough beer for the city revellers letting off steam, or just another day at the office for myself and my fellow professionals. But, as I stroll through the buzzing throng on a bright summer morning with the prospect of a day on the blustery Solent ahead of me I think: what an office!

EVENT

*Skandia Life
Cowes Week*

ADDRESS

*Cowes Week
18 Bath Road
Isle of Wight
PO31 7QN*

EVENT DATE

4th - 11th August 2001

WINNERS IN 2000

TICKETS & INFORMATION

020 7289 1864
Sportsworld Hospitality Line
01235 555844

WEB SITES

www.cowesweek.co.uk

For Hotel, Weather,
Travel Directions and
Additional Information
Visit
www.thesportingseason.com

NAUTICA

Pedigree Burghley Horse Trials

LORNA CLARKE - *British Three-Day Event Champion and BBC Commentator*

Burghley is one of the top, if not the top equestrian three-day event in the world. The sport of three-day eventing started in the early 1900's and originated from the military. It is the ultimate, all round test of horse and rider. In its original form it was to prove that military horses could perform parade and ceremonial duties one day, go into battle the next and still come out fit and sound to continue in service following the rigours of the battle on the final day. These three phases have been translated into the dressage phase on the first day, the speed and endurance (cross country) on the second and then one round of show jumping on the final day, the basic aims being the same as in its original form. All three phases are of course performed by the same horse and rider and the event is strictly monitored with veterinary inspections throughout the three days..

It takes a very special versatile type of horse to compete at this level of eventing. Horses have to be brave, bold and have great jumping ability, they also have to be good movers, very athletic, full of quality and have sensible temperaments. Just like their riders, they love the sport.

Burghley, which has hosted both World and European Championships on more than one occasion has been 'the happy hunting ground' for so many. Set in the most glorious countryside with the magnificent house in the background, the undulating parkland lends itself to a wonderful variety of cross-country fences. All solid and beautifully constructed using natural features of the land from the 'trout hatchery' (jumping into, through and out of water) to Capability Brown's road crossing (a steep drop and slide down to the road and back up the other side). There is something for everyone at Burghley but most of all, the challenge for the competitors! Horses and riders have to be extremely fit as prior to the cross-country itself, they have done twelve miles of 'roads and tracks'. This is taken at a trot speed round the perimeter area of the Burghley Estate plus over two miles of steeplechase at a good point to point gallop

performed round the Burghley Golf Course (sacrilege to some!). Then the horses have a ten minute break where they are again inspected by a veterinary panel before starting out on the final four and a half mile cross country course over approximately thirty two fences.

Being the ultimate test of horse and rider obviously takes a great deal of time, effort and money to get a horse to the standard required for such an event. There are also very strict qualifications for both horses and riders before they are allowed to enter. Horses are not allowed to start eventing at any level before they are five years old. They then start in novice one-day events and gradually build up through novice, intermediate and finally advanced one and three-day events before they can compete at a 'four star' (top level) event such as Burghley of which there are only four or five in the world. So by the time a horse gets to Burghley it will probably have taken three years of training to get him 100% fit and confident and just reaching the pinnacle of his career.

Apart from the thrills and spills of the cross-country, Burghley has so much else to offer. The magnificent house, an Aladdin's Cave of Art and Antiques is open to the public, the tented village with over three hundred exhibits sells everything from diamonds at Aspreys to green Wellington Boots and dogs beds. For the country lovers it is a wonderful day out just walking in one of Britain's loveliest and unspoilt country estates.

EVENT

Pedigree
Burghley Horse Trials

ADDRESS

Burghley Park
Near Stamford
Lincolnshire
PE9 2LH

EVENT DATE

30th August - 2nd September
2001

WINNERS IN 2000

Andrew Nicholson on
Mr Smiffy - N.Z

TICKETS & INFORMATION

01933 304744 from 1st May

Sportsworld Hospitality Line
01235 555844

WEB SITES

www.burghleyhorse.co.uk

For Hotel, Weather,
Travel Directions and
Additional Information
Visit
www.thesportingseason.com

The *Ryder* Cup

PETER ALLISS - *Former Ryder Cup Player and BBC Golfing Commentator*

My father Percy and I have been privileged, fortunate, honoured to have played in many Ryder Cup teams. The early rules of qualification were that you had to be born and be resident within the United Kingdom, which ruled out my father and Henry Cotton, who were both professional abroad from 1926 to 1931. Even so, we got into double figures and were unique in being the only father and son combination ever to have played in the matches until Antonio and Ignacio Carrido came along in the late 90s.

In a way I'm sad that the matches now have become ALMOST a monster. I suppose it's the passing of time, progress, moving on, changes in fashion that have brought about this sad reflection of mine, but I feel it is true.

Having said that, the excitement generated by today's matches is almost gladiatorial, that's not to say they weren't exciting and meaningful in days gone by. Contrary to some belief, the matches didn't come alive with the change of rules allowing Continental players to be eligible for the team, although having their extra skills and winning the matches obviously added a different perspective. It seems ridiculous to say that perhaps too much money is generated from these matches today, but that would appear to be the case. Professionals on both sides have been asking questions for a number of years as to where the profits go. Why should the two Associations (the European and the US PGAs) take all the money? It's always interesting to ask where the money goes, the balance sheets never seem to totally reflect where it has gone.

Over the last 15 years there have been some rather ugly moments in the Ryder Cup which, because of the increase in media attention, is blown out of all proportion and carried on for months, sometimes years, whereas our spats of years ago were only two day wonders. I suppose these relatively modern problems can be put down to a need of times with Paul Azinger from the United States and Seve Ballesteros from Europe. Their golfing feuds were numerous and, on occasion, bordering on the bitter.

You could point the finger at many people to say why the matches have lost (as far as I'm concerned) that certain SOMETHING. The desire to win at all costs is very prevalent, the fact that the money must be made, the fact that the players no longer wish to be involved in any of the off course activities, although they begrudgingly go to a couple of dinners, but they want to know why we should put ourselves out for any other reason. All these things have attributed to an atmosphere which, on occasion, you could cut with a knife.

Much fancy language is used about the quality of the game, the competition between Europe and the United States, a lot of waffle is bandied about and yet, for my money, it's still one of the world's greatest sporting events. Remember, it's only in the UK every four years, but I hope that this year, when the matches are played in September at the Belfry, there will be golf of the highest quality, enlightened crowds watching the golf, the game played within the true spirit that we of a certain age know it generates. I am slightly fearful that certain events may happen again. It all depends on how the players conduct themselves and the manners of those in charge of security and organisation.

The major part of me wants this to be a stunning Ryder Cup, played in good weather on a course with which I am very familiar, for it to be decided by brilliant play and not sad mistakes, mistakes bring false sympathy and gloating which, in turn, can lead to bad fan behaviour and animosity between players and would not please Samuel Ryder and those responsible for bringing this wonderful sporting occasion to a world stage.

EVENT

The Ryder Cup

ADDRESS

DeVere Belfry Golf Club
Litchfield Road
Wishaw
North Warwickshire
B76 9PR

EVENT DATE

28th - 30th September 2001

CURRENT HOLDERS

U.S.A.

TICKETS & INFORMATION

01782 741957

Sportsworld Hospitality Line
01235 555844

WEB SITES

www.europeantour.com

For Hotel, Weather,
Travel Directions and
Additional Information
Visit
www.thesportingseason.com

INKERMAN

Corporate and Private Gifts and Trophies

Inkerman is one of the leading corporate gift companies in the UK with a reputation for stylish, smart, fun and functional presents.
We specialise in providing team and individual prizes and trophies for a wide range of sporting and corporate events.

Contact us for a copy of our brochure or to discuss your event requirements.

Inkerman (London)
Telephone 020 7938 2300 Fax 020 7460 6622 E-mail sales@inkerman.co.uk
visit www.inkerman.co.uk

St Andrews
Cornerstone of The Alfred Dunhill Links Championship

COLIN MONTGOMERIE - *Record Breaking European Order of Merit Champion*

St Andrews, even to an untrained eye, is a truly remarkable place. Its history goes back a long way and the battles for power that went on in this small East of Scotland town, the birth of the University, the creation of the golf course, all have a wonder of their own.

The great Bobby Jones virtually "gave up" at St Andrews on one of his early visits saying that it was a ridiculous golf course, full of nonsensical holes and he would never darken its fairways again. Well, like many others, he came to change his mind and he won The Open at St Andrews in 1927. Jones so loved the place he once said that if you were to remove everything from his past except for his days at St Andrews, he would still have had a rich and happy life. St Andrews has stood the passing of time in a remarkable way, although I confess the 62 compiled by Curtis Strange some years ago, is still unbelievable.

The intricacies of the course are far too many to mention. It was always known as a golf course where you could hook to your heart's content, if you sliced, disaster awaited every yard of the way. But, in fact, I have not found that to be the case.

What is the charm of St Andrews? Many people believe the Royal & Ancient Golf Club of St Andrews, the R&A, own the course. Not so. The course is managed by The Links Trust, it is on public ground and actually the playing rights of R & A members are very limited. It is, at the end of the day, a municipal golf course, open for just over 300 days per year. It is remarkable how visitors flock from the four corners of the golfing world to visit St Andrews. I often wonder what they think of it when they see it for the first time. Likewise, I wonder what the members think of them as they sit in the great window looking out on the course at the various swings and strokes of sometimes, some very tired golfers!!

St Andrews will, hopefully, always remain St Andrews and avoid the pitfalls of modernising for the sake of it. Can you imagine if the Valley of Sin at the 18th was turned into a water hazard, the Swilken Burn enlarged and swept round to encircle the 1st green?

One of the great joys of St Andrews is its character. One of its delights that not many people have enjoyed is the fact the course can be played backwards. Yes, backwards! How? you ask, well from the 1st tee to the 17th green , the 18th tee to the 16th green and so on and so on. And would you believe it, it is an excellent course from that direction and up until fairly recently was always played that way round for a month in the winter. But one thing I have noticed, it is quite remarkable when looking back up the hole you have just played how often you can see bunkers you never noticed when you were playing it down, now was that by accident or by design? All I know is that from an architectural point of view many of the bunkers at St Andrews are magnificently made and strategically placed.

Some players can argue that it is "unfair" in places. Well - perhaps it is but surely that was what the game of golf was all about years ago. Skill, courage, nerve and a bit of chance. The modern game tries to eliminate chance but I don't think that will ever happen at St Andrews and the game of golf remains in very safe hands. The guardians of "our game" - the Royal & Ancient and the United States Golf Association jealously guard the rules and dimensions of the game. Long may they survive, long may St Andrews survive. A truly remarkable golf course amongst a collection of very good golf courses and quite unlike any other of the great golfing venues around the world. Everyone wants to play on the Old Course and no matter how good the others may be, it is the Old that gets most, if not all, the attention. In some strange way this is perhaps how it should be.

The inaugural Alfred Dunhill Links Championship will be played over each of the following three courses, with the final round being played on The Old Course at St Andrews.

The Old Course St Andrews
St Andrews
Fife
KY16 9SS

Carnoustie Golf Links
Links Parade
Carnoustie
DD7 7JE

Kingsbarns Golf Links
Kingsbarns
Fife
KY16 8QD

EVENT

The Alfred Dunhill
Links Championship

ADDRESS

See Left

EVENT DATE

18th - 21st October 2001

WINNERS IN 2000

TICKETS & INFORMATION

01344 840400

Sportsworld Hospitality Line
01235 555844

WEB SITES

www.europeantour.com

For Hotel, Weather,
Travel Directions and
Additional Information
Visit
www.thesportingseason.com

Sport In Your Area

For information about playing, coaching and all sporting facilities in your area please contact:

Sport England   020 7273 1500
                                     www.english.sports.gov.uk

Sports Council for Wales   029 2030 0500
                                     www.sports-council-wales.co.uk

Sport Scotland   0131 317 7200
                                     www.sporstcouncil.org.uk

Sports Council for
Northern Ireland   028 9038 1222
                                     www.sportni.org.uk

Photographers Credits

Shaun Botterill

Ben Bradford

Clive Brunskill

Simon Bruty

David Cannon

Graham Chadwick

Russell Cheyne

Chris Cole

Phil Cole

Michael Cooper

J.D.Cuban

Tony Duffy

Stu Forster

John Gighigi

Laurence Griffiths

Julian Herbert

Mike Hewitt

Harry How

Rusty Jarrett

Ross Kinnaird

Alex Livesey

Jean-Marc Loubat

Bob Martin

Clive Mason

Simon Miles

Stephen Munday

Adrian Murrell

Steve Powell

Craig Prentis

Gary M Prior

Andrew Redington

Ker Robertson

Dave Rogers

Pascal Rondeau

Richard Sakar

Dave Sanderson

Jamie Squire

Michael Steele

Mark Thompson

Anton Want

THANK YOU

The

SPORTING SEASON

A
Celebration
of the
British Sporting Year
2002

Available
from
November 2001

The Perfect Gift